ANNUAL 1997

™ © LWTP 1992/93/94/95/96
Made in association with the Samuel Goldwyn Company.
All rights reserved.
Published in Great Britain by World International Ltd, Deanway Technology Centre, Wilmslow Road, Handforth,
Cheshire SK9 3FB.
Printed in Great Britain.
ISBN 0-7498-2805-6

Written by Alison Daniels, Martin Steale
Produced by Newsstand Publishing Services
Edited by Alan Young
Designed by Rob Sharp

Note - Play safely!
Gladiators and contenders have undergone considerable training - do NOT attempt to imitate their actions or recreate Gladiator events.

CONTENTS

WOLF

Some say he's a sheep in wolf's clothing - don't you believe it!

FACT FILE

Date of Birth: 30th September 1952
Height: 6ft
Weight: 15st
Chest: 48ins
Waist: 30ins
Eye Colour: Dark brown
Favourite Colour: Grey
Favourite Film: I haven't got a favourite as such, but I love all the swashbucklers
Favourite Actor: Errol Flynn
Favourite Actress: Julia Roberts
Favourite Music: My favourite musician is Johnny Gill and I love heavy rock, like Bon Jovi - it's good music to work out to

Wolf is one Gladiator who likes to have fun while he's training and his hobbies help to keep him in top condition between filming series of *Gladiators*. He enjoys rollerblading and a good game of tennis; in fact, during the last pantomime season, he could often be found on the court at midnight, playing a game to unwind before going to bed!

But Wolf's favourite sport is snowboarding and in the past, he has travelled to Los Angeles, Canada and Italy to try out their slopes.

"All of a sudden, it's in vogue, but I've been doing it for about four or five seasons now, and it's a fantastic sport," he says. "I saw it on television one day and thought 'That's for me!'. I'm a speed freak! I've got three different boards; one for freestyle, one for carving and one for full speed racing. I like bombing down a mountain at full speed and just being generally stupid!"

However, Wolf is deadly serious when he starts preparing for a new series of *Gladiators*, as many contenders know to their cost! His training schedule consists of alternate days of weights and cardio-vascular work and as the series approaches, he increases the latter to lose weight and get himself in peak condition for the Ultimate Challenge. After suffering a hamstring injury during the '95 series, he's now fighting fit again and according to him, "Three times nastier than before! I feel sorry for the contenders!"

We'd all agree with that, Wolf!

GLADIATORS

LIGHTNING

This Lightning strikes again and again!

FACT FILE

Date of Birth: 25th December 1971
Height: 5ft 7ins
Weight: 9st 3lbs
Chest: 37ins
Waist: 25ins
Eye Colour: Dark brown
Favourite Colour: Peach
Favourite Film: Forrest Gump
Favourite Actor: Steve Martin, Anthony Hopkins
Favourite Actress: Jodie Foster
Favourite Music: Michael Bolton

When Lightning strikes in the arena, the blonde Gladiator makes it all look deceptively easy as she beats her contenders, but like the other Gladiators, her prowess when taking part in the Ultimate Challenge is the result of months of hard work. As each new series draws near, she steps up her weight training to increase her strength and muscle definition. "It makes me a little bit stronger to take the punches and the whacks that you get, so hopefully I won't come out too battered and bruised, and it gives me a little bit more shape," she explains.

Outside the arena, Lightning is a great animal lover and surprisingly, her favourite animals are gorillas. "They look so cuddly!" she says. "They have sweet little faces that make them look so innocent. I adopted a gorilla under a scheme run by the Dian Fossey Fund, where you send off some money which goes to looking after one and you get a T-shirt and a picture of it. I also collect gorilla toys and I've got quite a few gorilla documentaries on video."

But while Lightning loves cuddly, fluffy animals, she cannot bear snakes! "During a PA last year, Cobra and I had to pose with a python," she shudders. "They wanted me to kiss it, but I couldn't even touch it! The thought of it made me feel ill, because it looked so slimy, even though snakes feel quite dry. Call myself a Gladiator? I'm a wimp, aren't I?!"

We don't think the contenders who come up against you would agree with that, Lightning!

HUNTER

The perfectionist who aims to be the best!

FACT FILE

Date of Birth: 12th June 1973
Height: 6ft 3ins
Weight: 16st 8lbs
Chest: 50ins
Waist: 34ins
Eye Colour: Green
Favourite Colour: Black
Favourite Film: Braveheart
Favourite Actor: Harrison Ford
Favourite Actress: Michelle Pfeiffer
Favourite Music: Prince

Not content with taking part in the Ultimate Challenge on TV, when Hunter does his training, he pits himself against the best. By climbing, running and body building with trainers who are experts in their field, he adds a competitive edge to his work-outs.

"It makes me train harder," he explains. "If you're in the body building gym and you're the strongest there, it doesn't really give you an incentive to get better, so I have a good team of people behind me."

Hunter prides himself on his strength as an all-rounder in the *Gladiators* events, but he feels that there is still room for improvement.

"I don't want to be able to do just one event," he says. "I try to be able to do every event, although there are still a few events where I'm not as good as I'd like to be. But every time you get good at the ones you've got, the producers hit you with a couple of new events!"

As well as taking part in *Gladiators*, Hunter really enjoys working with children on the *Train To Win* shows. "It's fantastic!" he enthuses. "We compete in the shows and we present them as well, which is great fun for us because we don't get that much chance to actually talk behind the mic. The kids are awesome! They're very capable athletes and no doubt there are some little Gladiators in the making!"

HOW TO BE A CONTENDER

There are several steps involved in becoming a contender on Gladiators

Anyone who fancies their chances on the Ultimate Challenge has to first undergo a rigorous series of tests before they can be considered for entry. To begin with, they must be very fit. All the Gladiators agree that every year the contenders make their job harder because they just keep getting better. They have all studied the show, know the events inside out and have adapted their personal training to fit in with the Ultimate Challenge.

Once the would-be contenders have applied to go on *Gladiators* they are invited to a selection session where they undergo a series of tests to check their strength, stamina and general fitness.

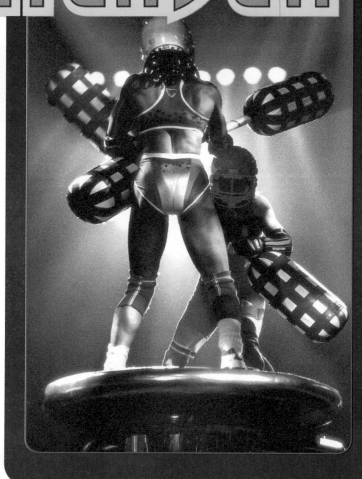

1. RUNNING

All contenders have to run on a treadmill for 800 metres. Women have three minutes to complete the distance, men have two minutes 30 seconds. Failure to complete this task results in instant elimination. But if the contender is successful, he or she gets two minutes rest before moving on to the next test.

2. PULL-UPS

Each contender has to hang by their arms from a horizontal bar with underhand grip, and pull their body up so that their chin is above the bar, then lower themselves again. They wait for five seconds then repeat the exercise. The women must do this five times, the men ten. They then rest for one minute.

3. OVERHEAD MONKEY LADDER FOLLOWED BY ROPE CLIMB

The contenders must traverse the 15ft long monkey ladder (like the one in *Pursuit*), climb the rope at the far end and then carefully lower themselves. They are not allowed to slide down the rope. Women do this exercise once and have one minute in which to complete it. Men have to climb and descend the rope twice, again within one minute. No-one is allowed to rest between the ladder and the rope.

4. PUGIL STICKS

Contenders are paired off and then have to fight each other as in *Duel*, to test their aggression. First one contender will attack for 30 seconds while his or her opponent defends themself. Then the positions are reversed. Both

contenders attack each other. They are allowed 30 seconds to rest between bouts.

Even if they pass all these tests, there is still only a limited amount of space in the *Gladiators* arena. Judges decide whether a contender has reached the appropriate standard with the pugil stick. If they handle themself well and demonstrate good ability and a determination to win, they could still be in with a chance.

The final test is an interview in front of the camera. Some of the best contenders can lose their nerve at this point, but performing in front of an audience is all part of the *Gladiators* experience. A lively and interesting personality can be the only quality that gets them through this last test.

AMAZON

A born competitor with the will to win!

FACT FILE

Date of Birth: 1st November 1962
Height: 5ft 11ins
Weight: 10st 7lbs
Chest: 38ins
Waist: 26ins
Eye Colour: Blue
Favourite Colour: Anything pastel
Favourite Film: Field Of Dreams
Favourite Actor: Robin Williams
Favourite Actress: Roseanne Barr
Favourite Music: Bette Midler

Amazon found her first *Gladiators* series last year to be highly enjoyable - but she became extremely frustrated when she snapped the cruciate ligament in her knee during *Pyramid*, which relegated her to the sidelines for the remainder of the shows. "I was just beginning to feel that I was really happy there and to think 'Now watch what I'm going to do!' when the injury happened," she confirms. "I think you need a series to get into it - to get used to the events, and the crowd, and the running of the programme."

However, after an operation and intensive training to strengthen and stabilise her knee, Amazon is back in the thick of the action once again and proving to be a valuable member of the *Gladiators* team.

"The Gladiators are all individuals in the way that we all want to perform well ourselves, but there are many games where we have to back each other up, and I probably find them the most enjoyable, because I've never played team games before," says the former Olympic swimmer. "They're a good bunch and a great laugh."

Because of her size, she often finds herself on the contact events such as *Powerball* and *Duel*, and she admits that she enjoys engaging in combat with the contenders.

"I am naturally a competitive, aggressive person," she says. "I've been competing since I was eight years of age and I must admit in the year I had off, in between giving up swimming and taking up *Gladiators*, I did miss it!"

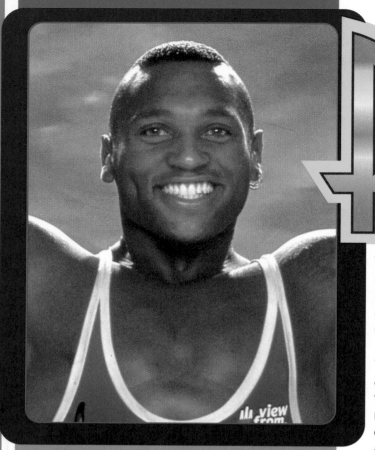

RHINO

He's strong and he's tough!

FACT FILE

Date of Birth: 30th September 1969
Height: 5ft 11ins
Weight: 17st 10lbs
Chest: 52ins
Waist: 32ins
Eye Colour: Green
Favourite Colour: Red
Favourite Film: The Godfather
Favourite Actor: Robert De Niro
Favourite Actress: Jodie Foster
Favourite Music: I'm into soul, rare groove, hip hop, swingbeat and jungle

When Rhino stepped out for the first time as a Gladiator last year, he was mentally prepared for the Ultimate Challenge - but he hadn't realised what an effect the encouragement of the crowd has on the Gladiators' and contenders' performances.

"There were so many people, and the atmosphere...!" he enthuses. "It was a bit much to take in at first, but all the Gladiators treated me really, really well and gave me a lot of advice, and the crowd were brilliant. Their reaction gets your adrenalin going and that's really good."

Because of his size, Rhino is an intimidating Gladiator at the best of times, but contenders' hearts must sink when they realise that they have to get past him in his favourite event, *Gauntlet!*

"That event suits me down to the ground," he chuckles. "It's a low gravity game and I can put my weight into stopping the contender!"

Rhino comes from a body building background, but as a new series approaches, he steps up his training by walking or cycling for an hour to burn off body fat before a breakfast of porridge and raisins. He also gets on the stepper three times a week, climbing about 1,000 feet in a session, and he sticks to a high protein, moderate carbohydrate diet.

However, every Sunday he allows himself to have what he calls 'a binge day' when he'll indulge himself by going out for meals, visiting the cinema, shopping and just doing whatever he fancies. This day of rest helps boost his metabolism, and not only is it good for him physically. "It gives me peace of mind as well," he says.

This Gladiator is well aware that life is no fun when it's all work and no play!

THE ASHES

In all, eight Gladiators made the trip down under to Oz - Warrior, Wolf, Jet, Lightning, Hunter, Nightshade, Vogue and Rhino. With them were four tough contenders who intended to show the Australians that it isn't called the Ultimate Challenge for nothing.

Male contenders Phil Campbell and Matt Beeke were both beaten by their Australian opponents in the heats with Australian Andrew Halliday the eventual winner. But star rivals Eunice Huthart and Kerryn Sampey distinguished themselves by making it an all-British women's final. Despite a tough neck and neck contest, Kerryn managed to overturn a repeat showing of the British Final (in which the same two women competed, with Eunice victorious) and finished the stamina-sapping *Eliminator* as the winner of *The Ashes*.

L-R Back Row:
Nightshade,
Warrior, Rhino,
Hunter, Vogue,
Fury, Vulcan,
Delta, Taipan,
Storm, Cheeta,
Tower, Condor,
Hammer
Front Row:
Wolf, Jet,
Lightning,
Cougar, Flame,
Blade

FURY

Fury is both fast and furious. Her daily routine for *Gladiators* training includes two hours of rock climbing and ring work. Not surprisingly, her favourite events are *Hang Tough* and *The Wall*, but she's no slouch when it comes to *Powerball* and *Pyramid*.

A former actress, the Fury of the arena concentrates her talents on just one thing - winning. "I love contact sports and competing to win, especially one on one," she says. "My strong points are speed, agility and the desire to win and not give up." When the Fury is unleashed, you'd best get out of her way.

VULCAN

Vulcan is big...and bad. He's Australia's answer to Wolf, the loose cannon with a short fuse. He hates to lose, and he hates losers. He can't understand why some of the other Gladiators will even consider talking to a defeated challenger.

At 6ft 3ins he is one of the most formidable Gladiators, especially in his favourite event - *Duel*. Despite his fiery temper, which Wolf encountered first hand during *The Ashes*, Vulcan has great respect for those who give it everything they've got. He manages his own gym and enjoys helping others to achieve their personal goals.

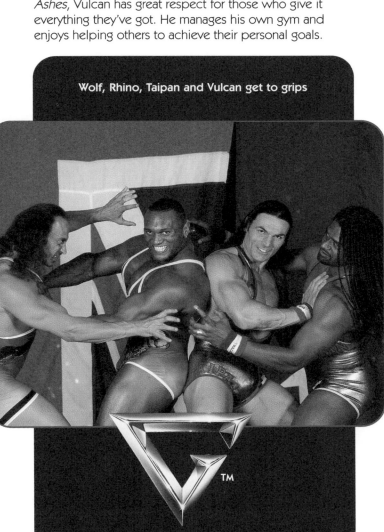

Wolf, Rhino, Taipan and Vulcan get to grips

Ashes winners Andrew Halliday and Kerryn Sampey

DELTA

Delta lives her life through sport, and when she's not pulling contenders off *The Wall* or hurling them from the top of *Pyramid* she likes to get her kicks with football and water sports. She enjoys the thrill of pushing herself to the limit and her sometimes demure look and quick smile hide a very competitive Gladiator. As the lady herself says, "I've got strength and I'm pretty aggressive mentally." A winning combination as many contenders have found to their cost.

TAIPAN

In Australia, a taipan is a huge venomous snake, and the *Gladiators'* Taipan likes to live up to his name. Despite his heavy 6ft frame, this former body builder can move like lightning to take his opponents unawares and deal them devastating blows.

Taipan is a man of few words who prefers to let his actions speak for him, although he will often psych out his opponents by facing them impassively with his arms folded and fixing them with his patented hard stare. "I really enjoy contact sports and competing to win," says the big man, adding, for those who hadn't noticed, "I am very strong and quick."

STORM

They say a Storm can blow hot or cold and this one combines the best of both. On the one hand she's easy-going and likeable and is always game for a laugh, even if the joke's on her (which doesn't happen often).

But don't let her happy-go-lucky appearance fool you. When she gets into the arena she's ruthless in her pursuit of victory and her karate training means that she is fast, supple and ready for anything. Once she's unleashed, there's no calming this Storm.

CHEETA

She's beautiful, she's tough and she's superbly fit. Cheeta's gymnastics training gives her the edge in *Hang Tough* and *Pyramid* but she's tough enough to handle the punishment of *Powerball* and *The Gauntlet*.

This former Australian Lightweight Bodybuilding Champion works hard and plays hard, hitting the gym seven times a week to ensure she stays at the peak of fitness. Her routine includes weights, power-walk, boxercise, cycle, treadmill and step class. She may be the lightest Australian Gladiator but Cheeta is certainly no lightweight in the arena.

Jet, Blade, Cheeta, Lightning and Vogue

Storm, Wolf, Vulcan and Lightning with presenters John Fashanu and Kimberley Joseph

TOWER

At 6ft 5ins, Tower is aptly-named. Despite his formidable size, he is something of a gentle giant, good-natured and easy to like, but don't take his smile for granted - one mistake is all he will usually allow. He may be big, but he's also very quick, as more than one challenger has discovered to his cost.

He's a former rugby player but in the arena, he is happiest in one-on-one events such as *Duel* and *Tilt*.

CONDOR

Condor is never short of something to say - especially when it's about himself. He might seem proud and boastful if it wasn't for the fact that he's so good. If a contender is lucky enough to get the better of him, he doesn't let defeat diminish his high opinion of himself. "For 60 seconds the challenger lifted his game to my level. Let the man enjoy his moment - it's not as if it's going to be habit-forming," he asserts.

HAMMER

When the mighty Hammer strikes, the blows can be heard all around the *Gladiators* arena! At 6ft 2ins, Hammer is a formidable opponent in any aspect of the Ultimate Challenge, but he excels in *Duel* and *Powerball* where this ex-rugby league star's size and build can be used to their best advantage.

Hammer takes the events very seriously, but isn't afraid to relax and crack a joke in between defeating contenders. He's confident but cunning, a combination which allows him to lull his opponents into a false sense of security before bringing them down to earth.

COUGAR

This Cougar is no pussycat! Among the many sports he enjoys, he's an expert kick boxer, and has won several titles in Australia. His small size and speedy reflexes make him a natural on *The Wall*, and he takes pleasure in pulling contenders off the vertical challenge.

He's something of a loner, and totally dedicated to his craft: "You keep putting 'em up and I'll keep knocking 'em down. That's why I'm here."

As a child, Cougar suffered from chronic asthma, but refused to give in to the illness. You'd never think it to look at him now, a fine example of what can be achieved through determination and training.

FLAME

Flame by name, flame by nature, the fiery redhead knows no limit where sheer physical power is concerned. She has been the International Federation of Bodybuilders' Miss Australia and when it comes to her greatest attribute, she has just one word to say: strength. Her favourite events are *Tilt* and *Duel*, which give her the chance to display her talents to the max.

When she's not striking fear into the hearts of contenders in the Gladiatorial arena, 29-year-old Flame is a member of the New South Wales Ambulance Rescue Squad - a Gladiator who fights hard, but cares too.

BLADE

This former Australian aerobics champion actually began her medal-winning exploits in the UK. From the age of 10 she was a member of the Great Britain National Elite Gymnastics Squad and represented us throughout Europe and Canada. But she didn't pull any punches against the British contenders in *The Ashes*. Australian *Gladiators* fans have long known that Blade is sharp, especially in her favourite events - *Hang Tough* and *The Wall*.

THE NEW EVENTS

Each series the *Gladiators* team try to come up with new and exciting events to extend the range of the Ultimate Challenge.

SUMO BALL

A seven foot foam-coated ball is suspended by a cord from the roof of the *Gladiators* arena. One Gladiator and one contender face each other across a circular platform with the ball between them. Their task is to try to push each other off the platform in whatever way they can but they are not allowed to let go of the handgrip on the side of the ball. They have 40 seconds to dislodge their opponent. If the contender stays on for the full distance he or she receives five points. If the Gladiator is knocked off, the contender gets ten points.

The mighty steel *Pendulum* ball measures 17 feet across and hangs about 25 feet above the ground with a safety net in case anyone gets into difficulty. The ball is surrounded by a cargo net onto which the opponents must cling. Gladiator and contender begin on opposite sides of the *Pendulum* and have one minute to duck and weave their way around the ball as the Gladiator attempts to grab the streamer attached to the contender's back. If the contender evades capture for more than 40 seconds they gain five points. If they stay clear for the full minute they receive ten points. Of course, they receive no points at all if they are caught.

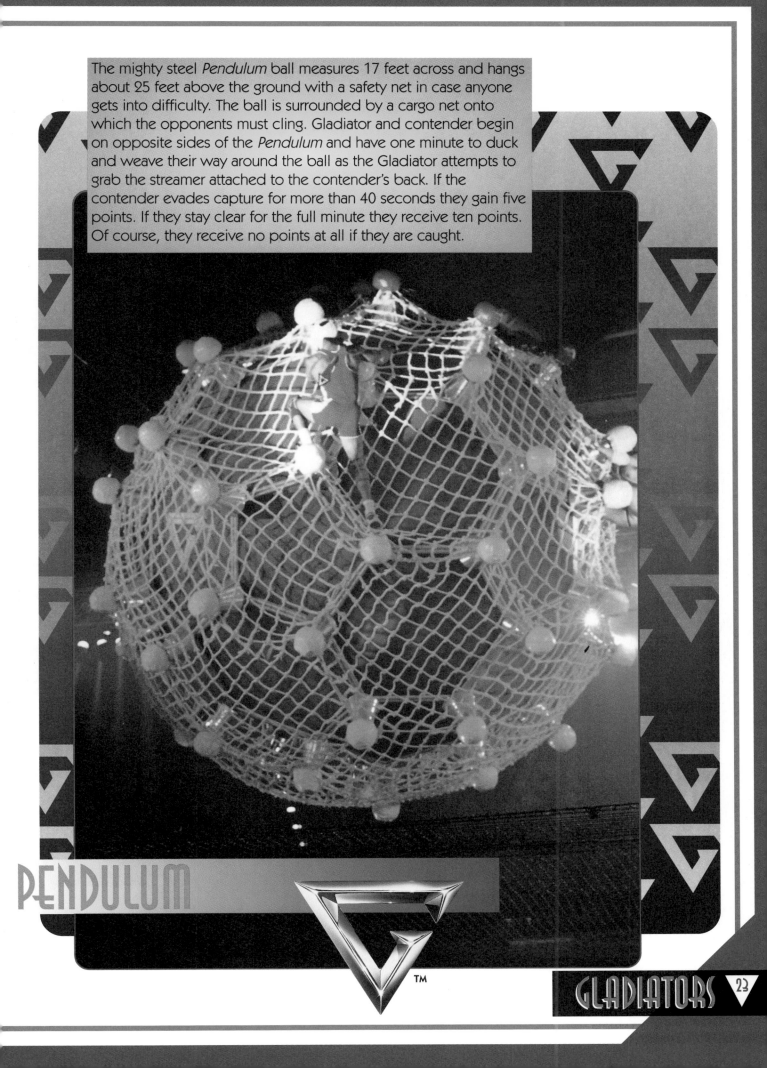

PENDULUM

THE ELIMINATOR

The latest series saw a change to *The Eliminator*. Now, as well as the hurdles, hand bike, rolling beam, cargo net, zip line, balance bar and energy-sapping *Travelator*, those poor contenders have to deal with *Spaghetti Junction*, a confusing array of scaffolding and bungee ropes which makes the programme's toughest event even tougher!

In a 20 foot diameter circle, a contender faces a Gladiator. The two are separated by a 'dog bone', two metal cones joined by a six inch rod made of very strong rubber. The contender has 30 seconds to use all their might to pull the Gladiator from the circle. If they succeed they gain ten points. The Gladiator can pull as hard as he or she likes but is not allowed to step out of the circle.

WHIPLASH

TIGHTROPE

Two identical ropes with one end slightly higher than the other are strung and tightened across the arena, 30 feet in the air. One Gladiator and one contender must traverse upwards along their rope to a platform at the other end. Once there, they use a zip line to bring themselves back down the rope to their original platform. The first to arrive gets to press the power button which releases their opponent's hand grip, sending them falling to the safety net below. If the contender wins, they gain themselves ten points.

A

A is for Athletics. All the Gladiators are first-class athletes at the peak of their fitness. And so are the contenders. Only the best can hope to tackle the Gladiators.

B

B is for Brawn. Although the variety of the events means that only the best all-rounder will succeed, a good dose of solid brawn doesn't go amiss when you're bashing away for all you're worth in *Duel* or powering your way through the *Gauntlet*.

C

C is for Cunning. In many of the events it's not enough just to be fit and fast, you've also got to use your head and employ some tactics. *Pendulum*, *Pyramid* and *Hang Tough* are some of the events for which tactics are essential.

D

D is for Dedication. Many come forward, but few are chosen, and it's certain that only those with the utmost dedication to their chosen task can make it to the final of the Ultimate Challenge.

E

E is for Excellence. Some are as strong as a Rhino, some are as fast as Lightning, some have the fearless determination of the Hunter and others have the killer instinct of the Wolf, but one thing all the Gladiators have in common is their ability to be the best. Excellence in all things.

F

F is for Fun. Despite the knocks and bruises, the gruelling training, and the disappointment of the many who must lose, the Ultimate Challenge is about having a good time, for contenders, Gladiators and audience alike.

G

G is for Gung-ho. Sometimes the only thing that helps the contenders as they battle the Gladiators is their determination to go for broke and give it all they've got.

H

H is for Health. Both Gladiators and contenders alike know how important it is to look after themselves - that means eating the right food, exercising regularly and generally taking care of their bodies both inside and out.

I

I is for Invincible. Despite their proven excellence in the Gladiatorial arena, none of the Gladiators is invincible. Contenders always have a chance, but it's tough going. It's not called the Ultimate Challenge for nothing!

J

J is for Justice, swiftly and fairly meted out by referee John Anderson.

K

K is for Knocks. There are more than a few of these on *Gladiators*, but there is always a team of doctors on stand-by to deal with any injuries.

L

L is for Leotard. *Gladiators* just wouldn't be the same without those stylish individually designed lycra leotards we have all come to love.

M is for Muscles. Something none of the Gladiators are short of. But it takes more than muscles alone to tackle the skill and might of the Gladiators.

N is for Nerve. When the lights are on you and the crowd is watching, you cannot afford to lose your nerve as you face the Ultimate Challenge.

O is for Organised. To compete with the best, you have to organise your time so you can get the most from your training schedule.

P is for Pantomime. At Christmas time, when the Gladiators aren't perfecting their craft in the arena, they take to the stage to prove they can be top flight entertainers and bring a smile to millions of faces.

Q is for Quality. One thing none of the Gladiators will compromise on is the quality of their perfomance. They always give their best, no matter what.

R is for Respect. Some contenders can get a little cocky before they get to grips with the Ultimate Challenge. But the Gladiators know how important it is to respect your opponent. After all, they've got this far, and that's an achievement in itself.

S is for Shades. Where would Trojan be without his trademark aviator shades? He'd still be a top Gladiator for sure, but he wouldn't be half as cool!

T is for Tough Guys. Nothing worth having comes easily in life, and the *Gladiators* Final is no exception. If you want to win, you've got to be tough enough to get through the gruelling training, and not lose your nerve once you're doing it for real in the arena.

U is for Ultra. Ultra-fit, ultra-competitive, ultra-cool. No matter what, the Gladiators take it to the max!

V is for Villain, and that's got to be Wolf. But don't worry, we all know his howl is a lot worse than his bite.

W is for Weight Watching. The Gladiators weights range between 9 stone 8lbs (Jet and Lightning) and 19 stone 8lbs (Warrior), but they all make sure that their weight ties in with their body shape and height.

X is for X-ray eyes, something many contenders have wished they had as a Gladiator closes the gap on *Skytrak* or *The Wall*.

Y is for Yard, and it's the ability to go the extra yard when necessary that marks out the true Gladiator contenders from the wannabes.

Z is for Zigzag. The fastest way to get between two points is not necessarily in a straight line, as contenders in *Powerball*, *Gauntlet* and *Atlaspheres* will tell you.

JOHN ANDERSON

He who must be obeyed!

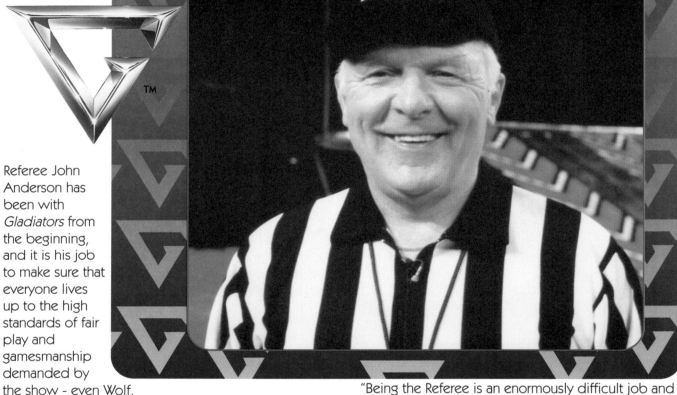

Referee John Anderson has been with *Gladiators* from the beginning, and it is his job to make sure that everyone lives up to the high standards of fair play and gamesmanship demanded by the show - even Wolf.

"As the Director of Training, I have a number of trainers to help me," he explains, "and we are responsible for ensuring that all of the Gladiators and all of the contenders are familiar with the games and activities they'll be required to perform in the competitions, that they are fit and able and that they are as reasonably well-trained as they can be in the relatively short time we have available. And while we're taking them through the events and other activities, we're reminding them about safety, the rules, the right equipment and all that kind of thing.

"Being the Referee is an enormously difficult job and anyone who thinks it isn't ought to have a try! When an event starts, you're conscious of the fact that both Gladiators and contenders are highly hyped, with 7-8,000 people cheering madly for their favourites, the lights, the music and everything that goes with it. But I have to keep cool, calm and collected in the middle of all this and sometimes it's even more difficult because the lighting is not wonderful from a visual point of view, so I have to concentrate totally on watching every move. I suppose you could say that the one period which is totally my responsibility is from the first whistle until the last, because during that period, we are in a world of our own."

even though they may be bruised and battered. They know the game has been run fairly, they know that my word is absolute law and I will not budge one iota, and they know that I have this passion for fairness. If it is shown that I have made a mistake, I'm willing to reconsider the decision - but after the event, not during it.

"The Gladiators are all very individual, as I am sure anyone who watches the programme will be aware, and they have their own particular ways of going about things. Some of them have, shall we say, slightly Machiavellian senses of humour, like the Warriors of this world. He looks like butter wouldn't melt in his mouth, but is always good for a laugh. Then you have the upfront guys like Cobra, who's a very open funny man - and then you have Wolf! The bane of my life! You have to keep concentrating on him all the time, because if you weren't watching him, he'd probably steal your whistle!

"What is wonderful about the *Gladiators* is that there is very rarely ever a show of dissent or bad sportsmanship. Everyone who enters the competition gives it everything they've got, but at the end of it, they shake hands, pat each other on the back and say 'That was a great competition',

"I go all over the country in my guise as an international athletics coach or as the Scotland Athletics Team Manager for the 1998 Commonwealth Games in Kuala Lumpur, and wherever I go, people say 'Oh, you're the man from the *Gladiators*!'. The excitement that's generated then is enormous and you can see that kids who are involved in sport want to know all about their favourite Gladiators. There are many, many thousands of kids who find their inspiration in the characters they see on the screen and want to emulate them in terms of being big, strong, fast and good sportsmen."

PANTHER

Beware the Panther's claws!

FACT FILE

Date of Birth: 14th October 1963
Height: 5ft 7ins
Weight: 9st 10lbs
Chest: 36ins
Waist: 24ins
Eye Colour: Greeny blue
Favourite Colour: Black
Favourite Film: Broken Arrow
Favourite Actor: Bruce Willis
Favourite Actress: Jodie Foster
Favourite Music: R Kelly

Panther is one of the seven original Gladiators who have been members of the team since the first series - but that doesn't mean she's getting too comfortable!

"Everyone is completely different because you get new challenges with the new games, and the contenders are getting fitter and therefore give you a more challenging outlook on your training," she explains. "Nowadays, I've incorporated climbing, circuit training and boxing into my training - and I took up rugby last year, which was quite funny because I ended up with a black eye! But it's all part and parcel of getting yourself highly tuned for the actual events; you've got to be fully prepared, because you just don't know what's going to happen on the day. And because the training is so varied, it keeps it enjoyable, whereas if you're only doing weight training and maybe running, it tends to get a little bit tedious."

Panther is aware, though, that mental agility and tactical thinking are as important as physical fitness when it comes to the Ultimate Challenge.

"The girls are trying to get together more as a team, so that we can talk about tactics and see what's the best way to train for a particular event," she says. "There's no way you can set a *Pyramid* up in your back garden to practise, so what we've come up with is running up the stairs at a stadium! You've got to think about how you can simulate the actual events."

However, the female Gladiators don't always take every suggestion on board. Panther chuckles, "In Hunter's case, he was pushing cars around an icy car park for *Atlaspheres* - but we thought 'No, we'll not do that! We'll leave that one to him!'."

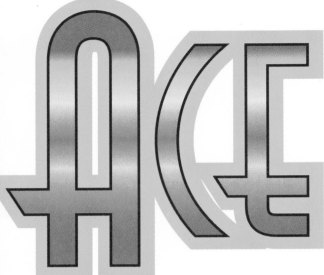

He aims to be the best!

FACT FILE

Date of Birth: 3rd July 1972
Height: 6ft 1in
Weight: 16st
Chest: 48ins
Waist: 32ins
Eye Colour: Blue
Favourite Colour: Blue
Favourite Film: Pulp Fiction
Favourite Actor: Gary Oldman
Favourite Actress: Pamela Anderson
Favourite Music: I like a wide range of music and I don't really have a favourite

Ace took the first step towards becoming a Gladiator by sending a photograph of himself to the programme makers - and five months later, they called him and asked him to attend a trial. An enthusiast of body building, boxing, rugby and running, Ace quickly changed his training schedule to prepare for his try-out.

"As soon as I got the call, I stopped doing all the power work that I was doing before and more or less dropped body building, and started doing loads of running instead," he explains. "I knew fitness would be important and although there are a lot of body builders out there, I thought if I wanted to stand out, I'd have to stay reasonably big, but be really fit. So that's what I did - and it worked!"

It certainly did - not only was he asked to join the *Gladiators* team, but after originally being scheduled to participate in three shows at the Wembley live event, his performance was so impressive that the producers asked him to take part in all seven!

Hang Tough is one of Ace's favourite events, but his ambition is to become a good at them all . "I don't want to be just stuck with a few events that I'm good at and then embarrass myself during others," he says. "I'd rather be good at all of them."

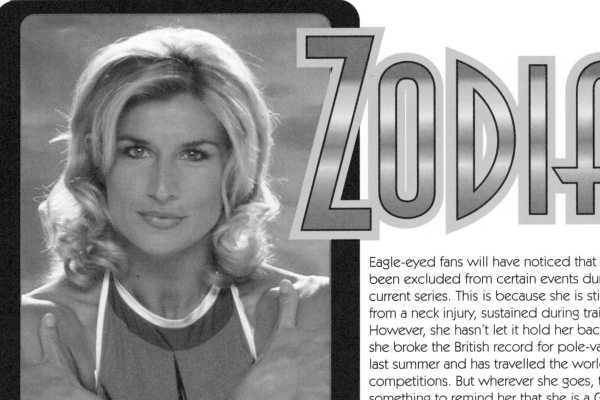

ZODIAC

Watch out for this high flyer!

FACT FILE

Date of Birth: 2nd November 1965
Height: 5ft 9ins
Weight: 9st 10lbs
Chest: 37ins
Waist: 24ins
Eye Colour: Grey-green
Favourite Colours: Blue and yellow
Favourite Film: Too many to pick one out!
Favourite Actor: Kevin Costner
Favourite Actress: Michelle Pfeiffer, Meg Ryan and Audrey Hepburn
Favourite Music: I have so many favourites, but I like Alanis Morissette and Celine Dion.

Eagle-eyed fans will have noticed that Zodiac has been excluded from certain events during the current series. This is because she is still recovering from a neck injury, sustained during training. However, she hasn't let it hold her back too much; she broke the British record for pole-vaulting twice last summer and has travelled the world taking part in competitions. But wherever she goes, there is always something to remind her that she is a Gladiator!

"*Gladiators* was on while I was training in South Africa at Easter," she laughs. "We went to a little restaurant one evening where they had a television set and so I saw myself on screen while in South Africa, which was really bizarre!"

Her pole-vaulting means that Zodiac is constantly training to maintain top levels of fitness, but as every new series draws near, she modifies her routine to include more exercises that are specifically designed to hone her skills as a Gladiator.

"In the winter, I do a lot of conditioning and endurance-type work," she says, "but as it gets nearer to the filming, I bring my running right down to sprinting over 40 or 50 metres, and everything I do is very explosive, very short and very fast."

On the whole, out of all the *Gladiators* series, she prefers doing the home series to any other. "Although the International series is fun, the team tends to get split up and I like it when we're all working together as a team," she explains. "My favourite game is *Pendulum* - no question about it! I always look forward to doing that one again!"

TROJAN

He's cool, but he knows how to turn up the heat!

FACT FILE

Date of Birth: 25th February 1968
Height: 6ft 2ins
Weight: 15st
Chest: 48ins
Waist: 34ins
Eye Colour: Green
Favourite Colour: Yellow
Favourite Film: Scent Of A Woman
Favourite Actor: Al Pacino
Favourite Actress: Julia Roberts
Favourite Music: Guns 'N' Roses and George Michael

Since starring as Action Man, Trojan has moved to Studio City in Los Angeles, to make it easier for him to pursue his movie career. But fear not, Trojan fans - he has no intention of leaving *Gladiators*!

"I definitely don't want to give up *Gladiators* ," he states emphatically. "There's nothing else like it - it's an amazing feeling doing *Glads!*"

In fact, now that he's living in California, Trojan finds it easier to keep fit than when he was residing in London.

"The nicest thing about being over here is that the gyms are the best in the world and the facilities are second to none," he observes. "And not only can you train in the gym, but you can train outdoors as well because it's so sunny. I'm also doing a lot of rollerblading, because they've got special tracks over here. Everything is geared around fitness in LA. You can go out to restaurants and order egg-white omelettes with fat-free pancakes, whereas in the UK, you could never do that, so it's very easy to watch your diet over here."

And since moving to California, Trojan has found that *Gladiators* truly is a world-wide phenomenon.

"I was on Venice Beach rollerblading and there was this guy in a restaurant looking at me," he remembers. "I thought 'Here we go - what does he want?' - and it was Giant, one of the German Gladiators, who was over here on holiday! So we sat down and had a drink together, and that was very cool. There's no escape from the Gladiators - they're everywhere!"

NIGHTSHADE

'Deadly' Nightshade never gives up!

FACT FILE

Date of Birth: 14th November 1960
Height: 6ft
Weight: 11st
Chest: 36ins
Waist: 26ins
Eye Colour: Brown
Favourite Colour: Black
Favourite Film: Demolition Man and Witches. Angelica Houston is an even more evil baddie than Wolfie!
Favourite Actor: Denzel Washington
Favourite Actress: Whoopi Goldberg
Favourite Music: That's a really difficult question for me, because I have 200-odd CDs, ranging from classical to spoken word. But I like Babylon Zoo for doing my aerobics to - anything that's got a good beat is always good for exercising to - and any swing artist

In some ways, the last series of *Gladiators* is one that Nightshade would prefer to forget - not only did she sustain a serious neck injury, but she was also dogged by a debilitating virus, which gave her respiratory problems.

"That really was the hardest series of my life to make," she admits. "It was a really, really tough year, but it just shows it doesn't matter how much your body hurts or how sick you feel, if you really want to get something done, you can."

But despite having had such a hard time, one of the few highlights of her year was the fact that her team won the *Train To Win* series. "My boys were really good," she says proudly. "They really came up trumps. I gave them a poster that all the Gladiators had signed, saying 'Don't be afraid to make your dreams come true', and I think they really did that."

That's a philosophy that Nightshade follows when she's not in the *Gladiators* arena, having long been involved in organisations which help people to make the most of themselves.

"I don't care what you do," she declares. "Some people are on TV and others are doing things which they perceive as less glamorous, but I always think that you have to do the best you can - 110%!"

By fighting her way back to the top from injury and illness, Nightshade is a living example that hard work and courage do pay off!

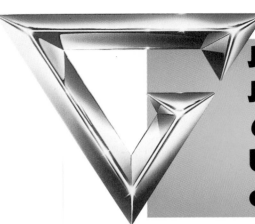

JOHN FASHANU

In the five years that he's been presenting *Gladiators*, John Fashanu has seen Gladiators and contenders come and go. But who did he think put up the strongest performance from the *Gladiators* team in the last series? He immediately jokes, "I think that Wolf did particularly well at being Mr Meanie! No, if I had to pick one Gladiator out, it would be Hunter. He has come on in leaps and bounds - although he's the baby of the team, he really has come of age. He's spent a lot of time training and he's looking fitter and sharper than ever. But I think the one to watch is going to be Rhino. He's a *big* guy!"

Speaking of Wolf, how does John feel about the fact that the Wolfman always seems to be giving him a hard time?

"Outside the arena, Wolf's the nicest guy in the world," John sighs. "He's a soft pussycat and he loves children. But once he pulls on that shirt, there's no-one he likes! You can see him pushing John Anderson in the arena and trying to fight him, and literally, an hour later, we'll all be sitting in the canteen, having a coffee and laughing. He's Jekyll and Hyde!"

After five years of *Gladiators*, John is pleased to see that the show continues to go from strength to strength. "It's been a long time, but people still seem to love it ," he says. "It's getting more and more popular all the time. That's good because we want to give enjoyment and pleasure to everybody, and while we're doing that, we'll keep on going . I hope we'll be going as long as Cilla!"

THE PRESENTERS

ULRIKA JONSSON

"I love presenting *Gladiators*," says Ulrika Jonsson, "because you never know what each series will bring. I love meeting the contenders. They are always a smashing bunch, especially the ones at the live shows; they have great enthusiasm and professionalism - and a sense of humour helps, too! I also love being part of a great team - and eating all that slimming food in the *Gladiators* canteen!"

Ulrika says that the ever-popular *Wall* remains her favourite event. "But I am now getting into *Pyramid* and *Gauntlet*," she adds. "*Pole-Axe* gives me butterflies just watching it, though! And with all the events, one always worries about possible injuries."

Asked to pick out some of the strongest performances from the last series of *Gladiators*, she answers, "Lightning once again performed well - and Zodiac too. Nightshade is still brilliant and Falcon came up trumps. Wolf is always bad - even when he's good! Hunter has proved he has very good all-round fitness - and Cobra keeps us laughing! The standards are improving all the time, along with the Gladiators' confidence and enthusiasm."

And like John, Ulrika is happy to see that the show continues to grow in popularity. "*Gladiators* has it all, for young and old alike," she explains. "It provides excitement, fun, fitness and glamour, and above all, it gives people at home something to aim for, which is important - because appearing on *Gladiators* is an ambition that it is possible to achieve."

GLADIATOR QUIZ

Pit your wits against the Gladiators in our fiendish quiz.

Answers on page 61

1. Who is the heaviest Gladiator?

2. Who is the oldest Gladiator?

3. Which country is Ulrika Jonsson originally from?

4. What is Cobra's mascot?

5. Which UK Gladiators took part in *The Ashes* contest?

6. Before she became a Gladiator, which sport was Amazon famous for?

7. Whose Gladiator costume features two hands?

8. Which Gladiator's trademark is a pair of sunglasses?

9. Which female Gladiator has the best record in *Duel*?

10. Who is the Gladiators referee?

11. Which Gladiator is also a writer?

12. In mythology, what is an Amazon?

13. Which male Gladiator is best at *Pole-Axe*?

14. What is the design on Saracen's costume?

15. How many Gladiators take part in *Gauntlet*?

16. Which female Gladiator is best on *Hang Tough*?

17. Who injured her back at the 1996 live event?

18. How many Gladiators are there altogether?

19. In which event can the Gladiators not take part?

20. Which event features giant swinging balls?

21. How many points does a contender score if he or she is knocked off their platform in *Duel*?

22. What is Wolf's favourite sport?

23. Which Gladiator is also a fireman?

24. How high is *The Wall*?

25. Which Gladiator used to be a bodyguard?

26. How tall is Nightshade?

27. Which Gladiator is a trained martial artist?

28. Who has two pet iguanas named Warrior and Hunter?

29. Who is Falcon's favourite actor?

30. John Fashanu is famous for which sport?

RIO

The newest Gladiator is determined to succeed!

FACT FILE

Date of Birth: 20th September 1971
Height: 6ft 2ins
Weight: 12st 11lbs
Chest: 36ins
Waist: 26ins
Eye Colour: Brown
Favourite Colour: Black
Favourite Film: Forrest Gump
Favourite Actor: Keanu Reeves
Favourite Actress: Whoopi Goldberg
Favourite Music: Massive Attack, Tricky

New Gladiator Rio is living proof that persistence and perseverance do pay off in the end!

The former Miss United Kingdom finalist entered a competition in the *Sun* newspaper to try out as a contender for *Gladiators* at the end of 1995. The makers of the programme were so impressed with her that they asked her to try for a place on the *Gladiators* team.

However, although she had been good at athletics at school and still trained with body building friends a couple of times a week for fun, her fitness levels were not of the standard required for the show. But Rio really wanted to be a Gladiator, so she gave up her job working for the Ambulance Service and spent the next three months training intensively for a second trial - which she passed with flying colours!

Rio made her debut at the live event at Wembley and confesses, "I didn't really know what to expect, because I'd not been on stage or competed in anything before. I was a lot more nervous than I thought I would be and I felt a bit out of my depth, but the other Gladiators were so lovely, they really made me feel part of the team. They were in the same position once and if I had any problems, I could always talk to them."

So far, she's found that her favourite events are *Powerball* and *Gauntlet:* - "Things that are physical and on the ground!" she explains. "I find the events in the air a bit nerve-racking, but I'm sure I'll get the hang of it with more practice. I can't wait to get stuck in again!"

The Gladiators have all had some special moments in the arena. Here are a few that they will remember forever...and a few they'd rather forget!

THE BEST...

VOGUE ™

Best Moment
"Meeting terminally ill children and making them happy."

Worst Moment
"My worst moment was my first go at *Pursuit* when my microphone got stuck. It was probably one of the worst events that I did during the entire filming of my first series and it went out as the very first show, when everybody who knows me would see it! Every time I went under the cargo net, my microphone kept catching on it and all I could see was the contender getting further away from me. I was not very pleased!"

HUNTER ™

Best Moment
"The first time I caught someone on *Hang Tough* was my best moment, because it's a hard event to do. I'd always wanted to do it, but I didn't get to do it until last year. Another great moment was the first time we marched out for *Gauntlet*, with the body armour on and the chant going."

Worst Moment
"Losing any event is always a bad moment for me, because I hate losing!"

AMAZON ™

Best Moment
"Probably my very first show, coming out and doing the intro. I very much enjoy being part of the team. When I was swimming, obviously I was always in a team and although you were individuals, you were all together, and I find that's very much the same with *Gladiators*."

Worst Moment
"My knee injury!"

WOLF ™

Best Moment
"We did the combined Armed Forces programme, taking on the Navy, Army and Air Force, and I finished one *Pyramid* and then straight away had to start the next one, but I stopped both guys, whereas the other contenders managed to get up, so that was quite an achievement for me."

Worst Moment
"On *Hang Tough*, during the Australian *Ashes*, I caught each guy on the rings straight away and each time, I fell off. That was terrible! We use metal rings, so when we give our contenders a tag, they're not going to stay on long, but the Australians have got wooden rings, and you can stay on there all day long, but I completely forgot that. As I tagged them, thinking they were going to come flying off with me, they're hanging on to the wooden ring like they're stuck on there with superglue! What I should have done was to climb up them and pull their fingers back. A lesson was learnt there: don't underestimate people on wooden rings!"

RHINO ™

Best Moment
"Winning *Whiplash* for the first time because I didn't really have a clue what I was doing!"

Worst Moment
"Stepping off *Duel* in Australia last year, on my first time up there. I hit the guy and then stepped back - and totally stepped off it! I'm a good actor, so in front of the camera, I was congratulating him and telling him he deserved it, but to myself, on the way down, I was thinking, 'Oh my gosh!'"

AND THE WORST

RIO

Best Moment

"I like the feeling of leading everyone out for *Gauntlet* because that's the one where you really feel part of a team."

Worst Moment

"Falling off *Hang Tough* during the live event."

COBRA

Best Moment

"At the *International Gladiators*, after a good battle on *Hang Tough*, almost the whole arena were going, 'Co-bra, Co-bra!', which was really good. It was an ego boost and very flattering."

Worst Moment

"I didn't practise *Pole-axe* at all last year because I didn't think I would be doing it, but the first show, they said 'You're going up *Pole-axe* today, Cobra!' and I got beaten by both guys - surprise! Old Fashanu was saying, 'You're getting a bit old for this, aren't you, mate?' and all the kids afterwards were saying 'You were useless on *Pole-axe*!', but you just have to swallow it because you can't come out with an excuse."

LIGHTNING

Best Moment

"I can't really say, because I like everything about being a Gladiator. You get to travel , meet lots of people and you get to compete. Obviously, I'm a very competitive person - I like it when I win!"

Worst Moment

"Whenever I get injured. That really drags you down, because you've got so many more shows to do and it limits you as to what you can do, so you can't push yourself as much as you want to."

REBEL

Best Moment

"Doing *Powerball* for the first time. It's a team event and when everything goes well, everyone gets a real good buzz out of it."

Worst Moment

"When I was doing *Pyramid* on the first three live shows, no-one got past me. On the fourth show, I had 47 friends come down to watch me and I lost! I was devastated!"

ACE

Best Moment

"On the very last show at the live event, the other Gladiators initiated me! About 15 Gladiators were all together in the middle of the arena while the men were being given their trophies and I noticed everyone was separating from me and I wondered what was going on. Then I think it was Wolf who shouted 'Now!' and they all tore after me! I ran round the arena about five times, but John Anderson stood in front of me and blew his whistle and told me to stop. As soon as I stopped, I got jumped on, pulled into the middle of one of the mats and they poured water and all sorts over me! It was after that that I knew I was in and I felt really good!"

Worst Moment

"My first go on the *Pyramid* was pretty bad because we hadn't had much practice and I wasn't clear about the rules, but I wanted to impress everyone. I came running down the *Pyramid* with Wolf, stopped on his patrol level and as our men had crossed at the bottom, I had to cross him. But I wasn't thinking straight and I ran into him, which didn't impress him! And then I got my man but as he fell, he stopped on the step below, and the force of him falling threw me straight over his shoulder! So within about five seconds, he'd thrown me off the *Pyramid* and was at the top, pressing the button - and everyone was shaking their head at me! That was the worst!"

GLADIATORS 47

REBEL

Tough enough to go the distance!

FACT FILE

Date of Birth: 16th April 1965
Height: 5ft 10ins
Weight: 11st 2lbs
Chest: 36ins
Waist: 28ins
Eye Colour: Brown
Favourite Colour: Cream
Favourite Film: Lady Sings The Blues
Favourite Actor: Denzel Washington
Favourite Actress: Whoopi Goldberg
Favourite Music: Whitney Houston

Despite being a very fit person, Rebel discovered that she had to modify her training schedule to become a successful Gladiator - and she also put on a stone of solid muscle!

"In track and field, you're taught to stay relaxed and to run with no tension whatsoever," she explains. "But *Gladiators* is all about physical output and being strong and actually putting yourself on the line. In some respects, you have to put yourself back in your childhood days, when you played British Bulldog in the playground and threw your contenders down! But we are all taught how to take the contenders out correctly, to minimise injuries."

Like all new Gladiators, Rebel had to undergo an initiation test - and she was well and truly caught out by Lightning!

"When we were coming out to do *Gauntlet* during the live event, Lightning said 'Have a good one!' and she patted my face - but she had chalk on her hands!" Rebel laughs. "So when I ran out, I had this white handprint on my face and I couldn't wipe it off, because I had chalk on my hands as well! Ulrika Jonsson and John Fashanu looked at me really weird and I said 'Don't even say anything!'. I told Lightning I'm going to get her back so badly!"

WARRIOR

The biggest Gladiator of them all!

FACT FILE

Date of Birth: 30th December 1960
Height: 6ft 5ins
Weight: 19st 10lbs
Chest: 55ins
Waist: 38ins
Eye Colour: Greeny-blue
Favourite Colour: Blue
Favourite Film: Predator
Favourite Actor: Arnold Schwarzenegger, Robert De Niro and Jack Nicholson
Favourite Actress: Sigourney Weaver
Favourite Music: Elton John, Seal

Warrior has had a busy year, moving to a bigger home in his native Cheshire. "The house is looking really well now," he enthuses. "I've got a great games room, with snooker table, pool table and darts, so I can have my mates round."

But, perhaps surprisingly, he will not be installing a gym in his new house. "I feel I have to get away from it all and totally relax when I'm at home," he explains.

Nevertheless, throughout the year, Warrior has been training hard to maintain his position as the tallest and heaviest member of the *Gladiators* team.

"I think the public like to see the big Gladiators - no disrespect to the smaller guys, but that's what they expect, really. I like to do personal appearances and there aren't many instances where the dads are bigger than me! That's just my thing and that's what I hope to maintain in the future."

And he admits that he still looks forward to the filming of every new series. "It's a nice time of the year for all the Gladiators. We're all together and we stay in a nice hotel - it's like a little holiday," he jokes.

GLADIATORS 51

SARACEN

The big guy with an even bigger smile!

FACT FILE

Date of Birth: 30th August 1963
Height: 6ft 3ins
Weight: 17st 4lbs
Chest: 52ins
Waist: 32ins
Eye Colour: Brown
Favourite Colour: Blue
Favourite Film: An American Werewolf In London
Favourite Actor: Samuel L. Jackson
Favourite Actress: Michelle Pfeiffer
Favourite Music: British soul groups like Truce and Eternal and I like bands like Oasis as well

The last year has seen Saracen working hard to get back on form after suffering two serious injuries in 1995, the first when he damaged his knee playing *Powerball* at the live show in Sheffield, and the second when he ripped a tendon in his arm during filming.

After an operation on his arm and a long lay-off from training, it's taken all his determination and commitment to get back on form for the latest series. "It is hard when you're sitting around, watching the other Gladiators getting on with it," he says. "This year, there's been a lot of catching up to do, because I was off for about six months and I only started training in February. I got back to where I left off fairly quickly, but obviously, I then had to surpass that."

And while many of the Gladiators have slimmed down to maintain a more athletic physique, this former body builder has been dieting to gain weight!

"I lost quite a bit of weight while I was off; I had to put on a stone and half to reach a reasonable weight and I will probably get even bigger," he explains. "Everyone else on the show seems to be getting smaller, for some reason, but I can handle the weight. I have no problems doing events like *Hang Tough* and I think weight is an advantage for games like *Duel*, *Powerball* and *Gauntlet*, so I'll stick to being a heavyweight!"

GLADIATORS 51

FALCON

She'll do whatever it takes to be the best!

FACT FILE

Date of Birth: 6th November 1963
Height: 5ft 7ins
Weight: 10st 7lbs
Chest: 37ins
Waist: 25ins
Eye Colour: Dark brown
Favourite Colour: Red
Favourite Film: Braveheart
Favourite Actor: Mel Gibson
Favourite Actress: Meryl Streep
Favourite Music: Gloria Estefan

Since last year's series, when Falcon found herself beating her contenders at events in which she was relatively inexperienced such as *Duel* and *Pendulum*, she has become determined to develop her Gladiatorial skills as a good all-rounder.

"Obviously, certain Gladiators like certain events, but it's nice to mix them around and occasionally do something that you don't often do - a lot of times you find that you quite enjoy it!" she says. "Hunter really came up trumps last year as a real all-rounder and he did well in all the events that he competed in. Although it's nice to specialise in an event, I think it's better, as a Gladiator, to be an all-rounder and to prove that you can tackle any of the events and do well."

Although Falcon trains with weights and aerobic exercise all through the year, when a new series of *Gladiators* looms, she becomes very inventive in devising a training schedule specifically tailored to individual events.

"If I feel I want to up my training for *Duel*, I'll maybe use a weights bar to practise different movements," she explains. "For *Powerball*, I generally get my son and my other half, and we'll go to a park or into the garden and practise dodging and tackling. And for *Pyramid*, I'll do a lot of hill-running. I'll do anything that I can think of that will help me with a particular event."

This is one Gladiator who is not only strong and courageous, but ingenious as well!

COBRA

The joker in the pack knows when to get serious!

FACT FILE

Date of Birth: 29th October 1963
Height: 6ft
Weight: 14st 7lbs
Chest: 48ins
Waist: 34ins
Eye Colour: Hazel green
Favourite Colour: Green
Favourite Film: Dumb And Dumber
Favourite Actor: Jim Carrey
Favourite Actress: Rosanna Arquette
Favourite Music: East 17

Cobra has his own way of making training seem like fun. When it's time to get fit for the Ultimate Challenge, he heads for sun, sea and sand and works out in Hawaii! "I do this back exercise which involves a lot of sand," he says. "It's a stretching exercise - you lie on the beach! I do hours of it every day!"

Joking aside, Cobra does a lot of running and weight training, to get himself in peak condition before the filming of every series starts. "Each individual event is only a minute long, so they're high impact, and you need a high level of physical fitness to last that five weeks of two shows a day," he notes, being serious for once.

"The live shows are a lot shorter, but we always use the contact games, so you have to be a bit more focused to avoid injuries. I've had most of my injuries in the contact games, but I've only got hurt from not concentrating and being a bit too passive - I'm always chatting away, while the contenders want to pull our heads off!"

Back home in England, Cobra has a training partner in his Alsatian, Rebel, who will 'sing' on command and stretch out a paw when his owner orders, "Give me five!" And when Cobra goes out on a training run, Rebel will accompany him, wearing a matching T-shirt! "He doesn't mind at all," comments Cobra. "But, of course, people round here look at me as if I'm mad!"

We can't imagine why, Cobra!

GLADIATORS 57

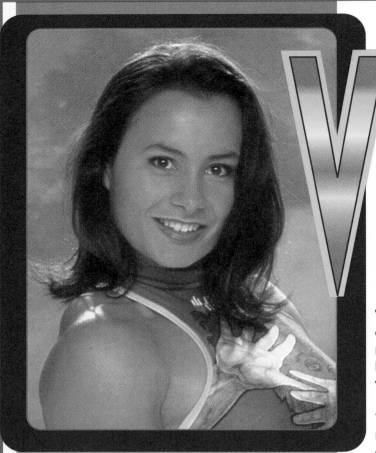

VOGUE

Last year's 'new girl' is now part of the team!

FACT FILE

Date of Birth: 19th March 1972
Height: 5ft 6ins
Weight: 10st
Chest: 38ins
Waist: 25ins
Eye Colour: Dark brown
Favourite Colour: Purple
Favourite Film: I like all sorts of films, but I recently saw *Babe* and that had major 'aaah' appeal!
Favourite Actor/Actress: Too many to decide on a favourite!
Favourite Music: Mary J. Blige, swing music

When she first competed at the '95 *Gladiators* live event in Sheffield, Vogue admits that she felt like 'the new girl', but now with two filmed UK series under her belt, as well as appearing in *The Ashes*, she's very much one of the team.

"I feel more of an equal with the other Gladiators now," she admits. "And I want to improve on the events that I do quite competently and get better at the ones which are a bit difficult to master.

"I really like *Hang Tough*, although I think everyone likes that. It took a while to get the hang of it - as it were - but I really wanted to do it, so I make sure I spend every possible moment practising that one. I also like *Powerball* - although it depends on the team that you get and the contenders whether it's a good game or not - and I think everyone likes *Pendulum*!"

When she's not competing in *Gladiators*, Vogue runs a business as a personal trainer, in partnership with her fiancé. Since becoming a Gladiator, she's been so busy that working together is one of the few opportunities she gets to spend time with him!

"My lifestyle has become particularly hectic!" she laughs. "I enjoy the Gladiators' PAs and I really look forward to them, because it's exciting going to new places and meeting loads and loads of different people, who are obviously pleased to see you. That's a really nice feeling."

GLADIATORS COMPETITION

Don't miss your chance to win these terrific prizes in our great easy-to-enter competition!

All you have to do is answer this simple question:
Which Gladiator's symbol is a horse?
...and then tell us which is your favourite event and why.

1ST PRIZE

Gladiators bicycle suitable for younger children

Gladiators bicycle suitable for older children (similar to one shown)

Fill out to enter!

Question: Which Gladiator's symbol is a horse?

Answer: Trojan

My favourite event is: Eliminator

Because: It is very exciting

Name: Sarah Gibbons

Address: 9 Cote Rd. Shawbirch. Telford Shropshire
Postcode: TF5 0NQ

Age: 6   Your height (to determine frame size of bicycle) 4 ft

Send your entry to: **Gladiators Competition,** Marketing Department, World International Ltd, Deanway Technology Centre, Wilmslow Road, Handforth, Cheshire, SK9 3FB.

Complete the entry form opposite and send it to the address shown, to arrive before Monday 3rd February 1997. Send a photocopy if you don't want to cut the page.

The sender of the first correct entry drawn on 3rd February 1997 will win a bicycle from Cycleurope UK matched to the winner's age.

RUNNERS-UP PRIZES

The next 10 correct entries drawn will each win a goodie bag featuring a *Gladiators* T-shirt from Charterhouse Holdings, a copy of Trojan's book, *My Life With The Gladiators* and *The Official Gladiators Training Programme* by referee John Anderson.

The senders of the next 10 correct entries drawn will win a copy of both books.

The next 50 runners-up will each win a Gladiators Fun Pack containing colouring and activity books.

ENTRY FORM
RULES

QUIZ ANSWERS

25-30 Gladiator
Hurrah! You're a *Gladiators* expert and no mistake. Well done!

16-24 Contender
Hmm, not bad, but you've still got to push yourself those last few hard yards to make it into the elite ranks of the Gladiators.

1-15 Wipeout
Oh, dear. You don't know your Wolf from your Panther, do you? You've got a lot of work to do before you can tackle the Ultimate Challenge.

1. Warrior.
2. Wolf.
3. Sweden.
4. An inflatable sheep.
5. Warrior, Wolf, Hunter, Rhino, Jet, Lightning, Nightshade, Vogue.
6. Swimming.
7. Vogue's.
8. Trojan.
9. Nightshade.
10. John Anderson.
11. Trojan.
12. One of a race of warrior women.
13. Hunter.
14. A sword.
15. Five.
16. Lightning.
17. Jet.
18. 18.
19. The Eliminator.
20. *Hit & Run.*
21. None.
22. Snowboarding.
23. Saracen.
24. 36ft.
25. Rhino.
26. 6ft.
27. Cobra.
28. Panther.
29. Mel Gibson.
30. Football.

GLADIATORS